The Big
Snow Leopard
Book for Kids

BELLANOVA

MELBOURNE · SOFIA · BERLIN

Copyright © 2026 by Jenny Kellett

The Big Snow Leopard Book for Kids

**Visit us at:
www.bellanovabooks.com**

All rights reserved. No part of this book may be reproduced in any form by any electronic or mechanical means including photocopying, recording, or information storage and retrieval without permission in writing from the author.

ISBN: 978-619-264-036-1
Imprint: Bellanova Books

Contents

Introduction 4
Snow leopard facts 6
Snow leopard conservation 66
Snow leopard quiz 70
    Quiz answers 75
Word search puzzle 76
Sources 79

THE BIG SNOW LEOPARD BOOK FOR KIDS

INTRODUCTION

The snow leopard is the most elusive of the big cats and is very rarely seen in the wild. Unlike other big cats, which mostly live in warmer climates, snow leopards thrive in harsh, cold environments.

Despite what many people think, the snow leopard is its own species, and although similar in many ways to leopards, they are more closely related to tigers!

Are you ready to learn more

about these beautiful felines?
Let's go!

SNOW LEOPARD FACTS

Snow leopards are one of the five big cats. The others are lions, tigers, leopards and jaguars.

• • •

Snow leopards are the only type of big cats that aren't able to roar.

• • •

The snow leopard is the national animal of Afghanistan.

Although their name suggests that they are closely related to leopards, snow leopards are actually genetically closer to tigers.

• • •

The snow leopard's scientific name is *Panthera uncia*.

• • •

Snow leopards have whitish fur with black spots on their head and neck, and larger rosettes on the rest of their backs, sides and tail. Their bellies are white, soft and fluffy.

Snow leopards are the only big cats living in Asia's cold deserts.

• • •

The snow leopard is also known as an 'ounce'.

• • •

The name 'ounce' comes from the Old French word meaning *once*, which was originally used as the name for the European lynx. Over time, the name was used for snow leopards.

Snow leopards spend most of their time alone and are hard to spot, which is why they are often referred to as 'the ghosts of the mountain'.

• • •

You can find snow leopards across central and southern Asia.

• • •

Look at a snow leopard's tail. It's very long! Their tails are almost as long as their bodies.

Snow leopards aren't the largest of cats, but they can prey on animals that are three times their own weight.

...

The fur on a snow leopard's belly is nearly 5 inches (12.7 cm) thick to keep them warm in cold, icy conditions.

...

Although they can't roar, snow leopards make a range of other noises, including growling, yowling, and meowing.

A study conducted by the WWF found that snow leopards were living at 5,859 metres above sea level, which is around the same height as Canada's highest mountain.

• • •

Sadly, there are fewer than 10,000 snow leopards left in the wild due to poachers and the loss of their habitats.

• • •

Because of their rapidly declining population, snow leopards are listed as Vulnerable on the IUCN Red List.

Snow leopards are a **monotypic species**, which means there is just one variety of them, unlike other big cats, which have several subspecies.

• • •

Snow leopards can travel in the snow up to 33 inches (85 cm) deep, although they often try to walk in the less-snowy paths of other animals if they can.

• • •

Most snow leopards weigh between 48.5-121 lbs (22-55 kg), although male snow leopards can weigh up to 165 lbs (75 kg).

In the wild, snow leopards live between 15-18 years. In captivity, they can live up to 25 years old.

• • •

Snow leopards have beautiful pale green, blue or grey eyes.

• • •

Snow leopards very rarely attack humans. There have only been two known cases where this has happened.

Snow leopards give birth in rocky dens, lined with fur shed from their underbellies.

• • •

Snow leopards actively hunt their prey and have been known to prey on domestic livestock in more built-up areas.

• • •

Snow leopards like to attack from above. They often hide on a rocky outcrop before ambushing their prey.

Although they are carnivores, snow leopards also eat large amounts of grass and twigs. They are the only big cat to do this!

• • •

Snow leopards have small, rounded ears, which help to prevent heat loss.

• • •

The favourite meal of snow leopards in Nepal is the blue sheep. However, the blue sheep isn't blue at all!

Snow leopards mostly eat sheep, ibex, marmots, and deer. However, they will occasionally eat birds and other small animals.

...

Snow leopards have wide, furry feet, which act as snowshoes to evenly distribute their weight over the snow and stop them from sinking in.

...

Snow leopards are mammals (like us humans), meaning they give birth to live young.

THE BIG SNOW LEOPARD BOOK FOR KIDS

In one night, a snow leopard may cover a distance of 25 miles (40.2 km).

• • •

The subtle markings of the snow leopard make it very hard to detect, which is great for stalking prey.

• • •

Snow leopards can jump up to 9 metres high! That's over six times their body length.

• • •

A female snow leopard is called a **leopardess**.

The main threat to snow leopard populations is humans. Poaching and the destruction of their habitats are causing snow leopard populations to decline.

Snow leopards are good swimmers, although they only do it if they have to!

Adult snow leopards have 30 teeth — the same as all big cats.

...

In cold weather and blizzards, snow leopards wrap their fluffy tails around themselves as protection.

Snow leopards run at an average speed of 48 km/h (30 mph), but they can go as fast as 64 km/h (40 mph) in short bursts.

• • •

The biome where snow leopards live is called 'taiga'. A **biome** is a collection of plants and animals with common characteristics for their environment.

• • •

The taiga biome is recognised by its long winters, evergreen trees, and lots of snow and rain.

The 12 countries that snow leopards are native in are Afghanistan, Bhutan, China, India, Kazakhstan, Kyrgyzstan, Mongolia, Nepal, Pakistan, Russia, Tajikistan, and Uzbekistan.

• • •

Around the world, there are around 600 snow leopards in zoos. Around 250 of these are in American zoos.

• • •

Snow leopards have large nostrils, allowing them to breathe in plenty of oxygen in higher altitudes where the air is much thinner.

THE BIG SNOW LEOPARD BOOK FOR KIDS

Snow leopards are slow and steady eaters. They may spend 3-4 days eating a single sheep, and they never leave any edible parts.

. . .

Snow leopards mate at the end of the winter season and give birth between April and June.

. . .

Snow leopards start reproducing at the age of 2-3 years old.

. . .

Young snow leopards are called **cubs**.

Leopardesses take care of their cubs all by themselves. The male snow leopard leaves immediately after mating.

. . .

Mothers feed their cubs' milk for about ten weeks. They eat their first solid food after two months.

. . .

When cubs are three months old, they start learning to hunt with their mothers.

. . .

Cubs become independent at around 18-22 months.

Snow leopards are **apex predators**, meaning they are at the top of the food chain and have no natural predators.

• • •

Although snow leopards are largely safe from predators, foxes often prey on their cubs.

• • •

The number of wild snow leopards is expected to decline by another 10% by 2040.

• • •

Snow leopards can purr when they are breathing out.

Like other cats, snow leopards use scent marks to mark their territory and paths. They will usually scratch a small hole before urinating in it. They may also spray urine on rocks.

• • •

After ambushing their prey from above, snow leopards kill with a single bite to the neck and then drag their prey to a safe place before they start eating.

• • •

Each year a snow leopard eats about 20-30 sheep.

A litter usually consists of two to three cubs, but sometimes it can be up to seven!

• • •

Female snow leopards don't always give birth every year.

• • •

Cubs are blind at birth, and their eyes open at around seven days.

• • •

A cub can start walking on its own when it is five weeks old.

The **gestation period** (time that a female is pregnant) of a snow leopard is 90-100 days.

• • •

After cubs leave their mothers, they may stay together with their siblings until they are more confident about being alone — usually for a few months.

• • •

Climate change is expected to harm snow leopards. As the Earth's temperatures rise, the tree line lowers, meaning snow leopards' habitats shrink.

In 2013, government leaders from the 12 countries where snow leopards live came together for the *Global Snow Leopard Forum* to discuss what can be done to help snow leopards thrive.

• • •

2015 was the *International Year of the Snow Leopard.* But, we can celebrate and support them every year!

The badge of the Girl Scouts Association of Kyrgyzstan features a snow leopard.

• • •

Although there is not much video footage of snow leopards in the wild, the BBC One documentary series *Planet Earth* featured some amazing footage. The BBC Two series *Natural World* also has an episode dedicated to snow leopards. These are both worth watching.

• • •

Snow leopards are **crepuscular**, meaning that they mostly come out only at dawn and dusk.

Around 60% of the world's snow leopard population lives in China.

...

The home range of a snow leopard living in flat, empty terrain is large — up to 1,000 square kilometres. However, they may share this space with several other snow leopards. In areas where this is a lot of prey, their home range may be as small as 30-65 kilometres.

The snow leopard has many different names across its native countries: zigsa in Tibetan, *irves* (ирвэс) in Mongolian, *bars* or *barys* (барыс) in Kazakh and *ilbirs* (Илбирс) in Kyrgyz.

· · ·

In 2016, researchers discovered that many more snow leopards were living in the wild than they had previously thought, which is great news!

· · ·

They may look large, but snow leopards are only around 2 feet (61 cm) tall at the shoulders. They are 39-51 inches (99-129 cm) long.

Female snow leopards are around 30% smaller than the males.

• • •

When snow leopards sense that humans are around, they become nocturnal to avoid any encounters.

• • •

Snow leopards are **opportunistic hunters**, meaning that they will hunt and eat whatever they can rather than being too picky.

Despite being the smallest of the big cats, they can hunt and kill prey up to three times their size!

• • •

When male and female snow leopards are ready to mate, they will leave scent markings around for the other to find. During mating season, as well as trying to impress their mate, they may even hunt together.

• • •

October 23 is *International Snow Leopard Day*! This day is used to raise awareness about the problems facing snow leopards.

Snow leopards are very hard to spot in the wild, but your best chance is at Hemis National Park in Ladakh, India. Here they offer snow leopard trekking tours, with all proceeds going to protect snow leopards.

• • •

Snow leopards can often be seen chewing on their tails, although scientists have no idea why they do this.

• • •

While a group of tigers is called an ambush, and a group of leopards is a leap, there is no name for a group of snow leopards! This is most likely because they never form groups.

The oldest known snow leopard lived to the age of 26. His name was Shynghyz, and he lived at Tama Zoo, Tokyo.

...

Sadly, many snow leopards are killed for their beautiful fur. Many countries have now made it illegal to import their fur, which has decreased the number of deaths. But, unfortunately, it still happens illegally.

...

The 2008 movie *Kung Fu Panda* features a snow leopard called Tai Lung.

Farmers often kill snow leopards if they are preying on their livestock. This is a problem that conservationists are trying hard to fix.

• • •

The documentary *The Snow Leopard Calling* won the top prize at the 2020 Kathmandu International Mountain Film Festival.

• • •

Snow leopards are a very important part of their ecosystem. If they didn't exist, the whole ecosystem would change — there would be many more herbivores roaming the land.

SNOW LEOPARD CONSERVATION

Snow leopards are beautiful animals that live in the mountains of Central and South Asia. They are in danger of disappearing forever because of things like people taking their homes and hunting them. It's important that we do something to help save these amazing animals.

Fortunately, many organisations around the world support snow leopard conservation.

Some of the most well-known include the *Snow Leopard Trust, the Snow Leopard Conservancy,* and *the Wildlife Conservation Society.*

These organisations work to protect snow leopards through research, education, and on-the-ground conservation efforts. They also advocate for policy change to protect snow leopard habitats and educate local communities about the importance of coexisting with these animals. Other organisations that support snow leopard conservation include the *Snow Leopard Foundation, the Snow Leopard Network,* and *Panthera*, a global wild cat conservation organisation.

HOW CAN YOU HELP SNOW LEOPARDS?

You don't need to be a scientist to help snow leopards! There are lots of ways to help no matter where you are in the world.

Here are a few ideas:

Learn about snow leopards: You're already off to a great start! The more we know about these animals, the better we can help protect them. Ask your teacher or a librarian to help you find more books and websites about snow leopards.

Tell your friends: Talk to your friends and family about snow leopards and why they are important. The more people who know about these animals, the more people can help save them.

Support organisations that help snow leopards: There are lots of organisations that are working to protect snow leopards. You can donate money to them or even adopt a snow leopard to help them with their work.

Help protect the environment: Snow leopards need a healthy environment to live in. You can help by picking up trash, using less water, and saving energy at home.

THE BIG SNOW LEOPARD BOOK FOR KIDS

SNOW LEOPARD QUIZ

Now test your knowledge in our Snow Leopard Quiz! The answers are on page 75.

1 How many teeth do snow leopards have?

2 Can you name five of the countries that snow leopards can be found naturally?

3 The oldest known snow leopard was called Shynghyz. How long did he live?

4 How long do snow leopards live for?

5 What is a female leopard called?

THE BIG SNOW LEOPARD BOOK FOR KIDS

6 What is the scientific name for the snow leopard?

7 What do you call a group of snow leopards?

8 Snow leopards eat grass and twigs. True or false?

9 Snow leopards are big cats. Can you name the other four big cats?

10 Snow leopards can roar. True or false?

11 What is another name for the snow leopard?

12 Why are snow leopards often called 'ghost cats' or 'the ghosts of the mountain'?

13 What percentage of snow leopards live in China?

14 What is the snow leopard's favourite food?

15 What day is International Snow Leopard Day?

16 At what age can a snow leopard cub start walking on its own?

17 How many cubs are in an average litter?

18 Why do snow leopards have such small ears?

19 What colour are snow leopard's eyes?

20 What is the main threat to snow leopards?

ANSWERS

1. 30.

2. Afghanistan, Bhutan, China, India, Kazakhstan, Kyrgyzstan, Mongolia, Nepal, Pakistan, Russia, Tajikistan, and Uzbekistan.

3. 26.

4. In the wild: 15-18 years. In captivity, they can live to 25 years old.

5. Leopardess.

6. *Panthera uncia*.

7. That's a trick question! There is no name.

8. True.

9. Leopard, lion, tiger, jaguar.

10. False. They are the only big cats that can't roar.

11. Ounce.

12. Because they live alone and are very hard to find.

13. 60%.

14. Blue sheep.

15. October 23.

16. At five weeks old.

17. Two to three. However, it can be as many as seven.

18. To prevent heat loss.

19. Pale green, blue or grey.

20. Humans.

Snow Leopard
WORD SEARCH

```
F D V Q A S D V Z V N F
G F D U V M A M M A L N
S N O W L E O P A R D R
H J G F D N S W D A H S
P C B B L U E S H E E P
T U V T R S G R V F J T
A B D Z B I G C A T E R
I S S S Y T R S S B S E
G H E D F H J E I F L S
A G F S D E H N A R X E
G L E O P A R D E S S B
J H D S E F D S A G H V
```

Can you find all the words below in the word search puzzle on the left?

SNOW LEOPARD   **ASIA**   **BIG CAT**

VULNERABLE   **BLUE SHEEP**   **TAIGA**

CUBS   **LEOPARDESS**   **MAMMAL**

THE BIG SNOW LEOPARD BOOK FOR KIDS

SOLUTION

		V								
			U		M	A	M	M	A	L
S	N	O	W	L	E	O	P	A	R	D
				N						
	C		B	L	U	E	S	H	E	E	P
T	U						R			
A	B			B	I	G	C	A	T	
I	S						S	B		
G							I		L	
A							A			E
		L	E	O	P	A	R	D	E	S	S

SOURCES

"Top 10 Facts About Snow Leopards". 2021. WWF. https://www.wwf.org.uk/learn/fascinating-facts/snow-leopards.

"Snow Leopard Facts For Kids - Snow Leopard Information For Kids". 2020. Kidz Feed. https://kidzfeed.com/snow-leopard-facts-for-kids/.

"Snow Leopard Facts - Snow Leopard Trust". 2021. Snow Leopard Trust. https://www.snowleopard.org/snow-leopard-facts/.

"50+ Facts About Snow Leopards". 2021. Owlcation - Education. https://owlcation.com/stem/Facts-about-Snow-Leopards.

"Where Do Snow Leopards Live? And Nine Other Snow Leopard Facts". 2021. World Wildlife Fund. https://www.worldwildlife.org/stories/where-do-snow-leopards-live-and-nine-other-snow-leopard-facts.

"7 Interesting Facts About Snow Leopards". 2021. Wanderlust. https://www.wanderlust.co.uk/content/facts-about-snow-leopards/.

Trust, Snow. 2013. "Group Get-Together In The Gobi - Snow Leopard Trust". Snow Leopard Trust. https://www.snowleopard.org/group-get-together-in-the-gobi/

"Snow Leopard". 2021. San Diego Zoo Kids. https://kids.sandiegozoo.org/animals/snow-leopard.

"The Snow Leopard Calling". 2021. Snow Leopard Conservancy. https://snowleopardconservancy.org/2020/12/30/the-snow-leopard-calling/.

"Where Do Snow Leopards Live? And Nine Other Snow Leopard Facts". 2021. World Wildlife Fund. https://www.worldwildlife.org/stories/where-do-snow-leopards-live-and-nine-other-snow-leopard-facts

"THE SNOW LEOPARD PROGRAMME". 2021. Programmes.Putin.Kremlin.Ru. http://programmes.putin.kremlin.ru/en/leopard/animal.

"Snow Leopard". 2020. En.Wikipedia.Org. https://en.wikipedia.org/wiki/Snow_leopard.

Pocock, R. I. (1930). "The panthers and ounces of Asia. Part II. The panthers of Kashmir, India, and Ceylon". Journal of the Bombay Natural History Society. 34 (2): 307–336.

We hope you learned some awesome
facts about snow leopards!
Which was your favourite?

Visit us at
www.bellanovabooks.com
for more great books.

ALSO BY JENNY KELLETT

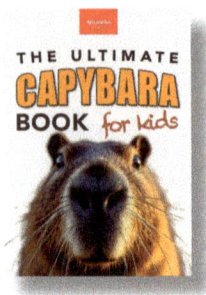  

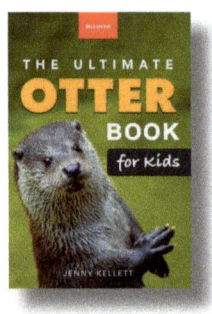  

... and more!

Available at

www.bellanovabooks.com

and all major online bookstores.

www.ingramcontent.com/pod-product-compliance
Lightning Source LLC
LaVergne TN
LVHW050136080526
838202LV00061B/6497